1-99

Who Goes There?

Fergus Allen was born in London of an Irish father and an English mother. He grew up in Ireland, attending Quaker schools in Dublin and Waterford. Since graduating in civil engineering from Trinity College, Dublin, he has lived and worked in England, where much of his career has been in the Civil Service. Having been Director of Hydraulics Research, he moved to the Cabinet Office and subsequently became First Civil Service Commissioner. He is married, with two daughters, and lives in Berkshire.

by the same author

The Brown Parrots of Providencia

FERGUS ALLEN

Who Goes There?

faber and faber
LONDON · BOSTON

First published in 1996
by Faber and Faber Limited
3 Queen Square London WC1N 3AU

Typeset by Wilmaset Ltd, Birkenhead, Wirral
Printed in England by Clays Ltd, St Ives plc

A CIP record for this book
is available from the British Library

ISBN 0–571–17782–4

In memory of my father and mother

ACKNOWLEDGEMENTS

My thanks are due to the editors of the following magazines, in which some of these poems first appeared: *Epoch, Grand Street, London Magazine, Poetry Review* and *The New Yorker*.

A version of 'Pond-Life' appeared in *A Parcel of Poems for Ted Hughes on his Sixty-Fifth Birthday* (Faber and Faber 1995). 'The Factotum' was a prizewinner in the Manchester Poets Open Poetry Competition 1955.

CONTENTS

Knight-Errant

No, I said *badinage*, not *bandage*,
Protective clothing for the psyche,
Not the dressing of bloodied tissue.
Behind my small talk can be heard
A constant jingling of the plates
That cover my vulnerability,
Each placed to parry or disarm
Projectiles like the sharpened word.

No, those are not the marks of rust.
This armour is meant to be lived in,
With its chinks and seams and weak points,
Which some days let in more than air.
I fancy myself on a charger.
Watch me prancing across the courtyard,
Coconut-shells on cobbles, sunbeams
Gilding my greaves and savoir-faire.

Getting out will be something else.
I seem to have grown into this panoply
Which cannot be moulted like plumage
Or left as one might leave a smart hotel.
I reckon to be hoisted by sheerlegs
Or, as in a forceps delivery,
Be drawn out head first, pale and curling,
A shrimp extracted from its shell.

Modern Times

My watch tells me the time in Calcutta,
So I know when the chowkidar of the Jain temple
Is on guard duty and sees the stars glitter
In the thousands of fragments of looking-glass
Stuck all over its far-fetched fabric
To signify preciousness and immanence.
Wrapped up in white cotton, pious and austere,
He measures out the night with his coughing
Until the next day's devotees appear.

I also have the time in San Francisco,
Where the animal klaxons on Seal Rocks
Bust the dawn wide open on the purply Pacific,
And the languorous heave of harmonics
From far-off cyclones stirs the kelp beds
Fringing Point Lobos.
                              Here, meanwhile, it's three,
The day moves on through quivering quartz
And the machinations of escapements,
Pallets that both connect and disconnect,
Taught to tantalize by gloating horologists
In the workrooms of Nuremberg and Utrecht.

I know a man whose friend has seen a *Zeitgeist*
Waiting its turn in the incident room
While its predecessor was put to the question,
Tied to a chair in what was once a nursery.
Even the children could see the joke.
But flora and fauna stick to their old programmes,
Mating at full moon, rising with the lark,
The owl perched aloof in the false acacia,
Shifting from foot to foot as he waits for dark.

Up and Down

Today I caught sight of the griffon vultures
Making for the land bridge and Africa —
A cue for me to assemble
And drive our sheep, crying and tinkling,
Down from the mile-high summer pastures
To the folds and knives of the valley.

I spend weeks up here on my own
Either side of the longest day,
My mind as empty as an airship.
The dogs run around and do the work
Or flop down on ledges of rock,
Watching for wanderers.

In my country we eat peas with a spoon,
We do not queue for buses, and the demand
For Western diseases of affluence
Far exceeds the supply.
The lammergeiers drop our bones
Out of the blue, hungry for marrow.

Stuck with half-exile and geology,
I have lost the knack of conversation.
Winters in the town are full of awkwardness,
Silence over backgammon
And jokes that pass me by
Screaming like swifts.

Last year in a smoky room I learned
That a fisherman on a visit
Had taken away my girl;
And the old man in the corner,
Curved like a sickle,
Was said to have minded flocks in the mountains.

Circus

Tumblers out of the ring, please. Thank you.
And now, against your disapproval,
We present our animal acts.
First we welcome Miss Maisie Hapgood
In the role of Hortense; our legendary
Duchesse de Mazarin (later of Chelsea),
Followed by Guido Malatesta,
Tyrant and attention-seeking rake,
Played tonight by the upwardly mobile
Herbert Greenhaligon in velvet.

See how they sidle round each other,
He on his roan, she on her gelding,
While Sousa music scatters thought
And the horses' ears attend to the cymbals.
It might be the dumb show of a feud
Or a ritual that goes with mating,
But the mirror-covered sphere of words
With its flashy circular theories
Has dropped from the canvas ceiling
And rolled clean out of the big marquee.

Wach them with eyes absorbent as infants' –
His seat, his smirk, his grand moustaches,
And her head, radiant and fragile,
Balanced on the rope-trick of her spine
As she holds the side-saddle pose
In her cockaded hat and gaberdine.
And the monkeys! – a sooty macaque
Leaps chattering on to Guido's shoulder
While an anxious capuchin in transit
Clings briefly to her blue-blooded bosom.

Around them performing poodles hurdle
Insouciantly through flaming hoops,
But the handicapped dancing bears
After a long night at the Whisky-à-Go-Go
Sorely need their sleep in the straw.
And fast through a tunnel of iron bars
Come the tigers, padding to their cage
To crouch on giants' painted furniture
And snarl and claw the air at threats
From a man with a bentwood chair.

A drum-roll signals the dénouement,
With Hortense translating to Guido's horse
And posing, arms outstreched, loving you all.
But the gross clowns have been sneaking back
To pour soup into their baggy trousers
And smuggle in the thin end of chaos.
Already the riggers are approaching,
Setting about the guys and turnbuckles,
Ready for the next date, Lord knows where —
Could be in the nebula of The Crab.

Too Much Gain

Lymph rustling in the privacy
Of semicircular canals,
Or cold air streaming off the mountains
To sift through buckthorn and jujube,
Or the exhalation of mules
Turning over infertile dreams:
I push through the flap of the tent
To shake off sleep under the colander
Of the still just night sky.

We rise early to load
The pack animals before dawn
And seat the women and their wool
And the half-made rugs and utensils
Over and round the creatures' backs.
The glow in the somnolent south
Rises from Shiraz and its sins.
We go there only for the mosque
And double-dealing traders.

Even now at first light
An unpromotable muezzin
Traipses off to the minaret
And flips an amplifier's switch.
A record of the call to prayer
Breaks over the flat roofs and laundry.
Even souls like oysters must shrink
Under the histrionics, fervent,
Raucous, with too much gain.

In the hills, too, the precepts
And aphorisms about God
Are swallowed whole, but here at least
We can focus and see for miles.
In summer the receding snowline
Discloses indigenous plants
Holding their own in a hard world
Where clear water slides over gravel.
  In winter we eat goat.

Foreign Fields

Round the converted fortress
Disjected barrels
Of Portuguese cannon
Lie amidst hawkweed,
Aligned as if to trip
Ancient historians.

In a space defined by boulders
Of nummulitic limestone,
Now half-hidden by osiers,
Rosemary and euphorbia,
Virgins once chattered and plaited
The still flexible grass-stems.

Across the bay are outlines
Of a ritual drying-house
To which their simple artefacts
Were taken by boat and pannier
For vetting by chthonic deities.
Observe the rope-marks on the bollards,
The initials chipped into the quoins.

Tickets for the tour may be purchased
From a lady with undulant fever
To be found under fluorescent lights
In the last office but one on the left
(Looking from the entrance on the Exchange).
Bear with her enlarged spleen, and do not smoke;
Her home life, if described, would wring your withers —
Her dementing mother calls her a whore.

The obligatory insurance covers
Acts of God, including impact from cattle,
But she cannot protect you from death.
Were it not for endemic leishmaniasis
The itinerary would circle south
To take in what is known as the Treasury,
Set in the marshes, and the bench tombs
With scribes and defaulters in relief.

But there will be no shortage of remains,
Broken columns and reassurances
About a sort of life to come –
Words on commemorative slabs
To help you feel you're winning,
The tittle-tattle of warblers
Restless in a smoke-bush.

Ornithologists, too, will be welcome
And provided with makeshift hides
To conceal their humanity.
Silent from long before cock-crow,
The patient and elect
May see the sunbird rise
Out of the flowering reed-mace.

Blue Sky, Dusty Horizon

Our men are stronger and more potent,
They dance at night and beget males.
Jolting through the mountains in diesels,
They can go without sleep for days.
They dangle guns from their loose limbs.
In war none can withstand their violence
And metaphysical excesses.
Their verdicts are cruel but just.

Our women, they say, are like goldfish.
In their tanks' privacy and darkness
They conduct their carnal researches.
Our sons are taken off for hardening
By their eighth birthday at the latest,
But our daughters learn how to swim
In the pools of their mothers' eyes
(We have a tradition of poetry).

Our priests are more like politicians
But sometimes sound off about God,
Calling on us for deeper sacrifice.
It's the old ones who cast the horoscopes,
Working nights, under the star clusters,
But their evasions and presentiments
Neither switch on the lights today
Nor tell us what we shall inherit.

Useful Transactions in Philosophy

Either you know the password or you don't;
Guessing is useless, guesses get you nowhere.
Sands of the desert! And God knows the language
Is hard enough to speak, let alone write.
When I approached the grille in the plate glass
The shy Jamaican shook her smiling head.
'Sorry, but that is last week's word,' she said.

Once or twice I was privy to the secret,
But not for long; and again there were knots
Of snake-haired girls whispering in the shadows
At the farther end of the classroom corridor.
In the financial district I looked down
From the visitors' gallery at the war
And camaraderie of the market floor.

At the theatre we often took a box
('Steering clear of infection,' said my mother).
Yes, champagne was provided for the coterie,
But I sat soberly alongside, watching
The golden apples fly from hand to hand
As *ingénue* Russian princesses played
In the walled garden where the pacts were made.

Impossible, of course, to speak with nabobs
Or reclusive grandees holed up in palaces;
For them belonging is part of genetics.
Acquiescence is looked for, eyes on the ground,
Just follow the trail of elephant dung
Along yesterday's ceremonial way
While golden boys and girls go out to play.

Near Naples

After the earthquake we decided to redecorate Hell.
  The walls and stone-flagged floors cried out for a face-lift,
  The frescoes of torments were behind the times
  And the macabre ambiance unsettled the workforce,
  Reducing output. We knew we could afford it
  And felt sure that tasteful interiors and pain
    Would cohabit well.

We first favoured polychrome mosaics of flowering plants
  (Creativity not being our strongest suit),
  Until our fancy lighted on painted stucco,
  With Nilotic scenes portrayed in a blue-grey mist,
  Or a naked wanderer in twilight, heading
  For a temple set among powdery trees,
    Campania in trance.

Then this seemed vapid, so we opted for an older style:
  Tall panels in black or cinnabar, with ochre
  In lieu of gold to simulate false perspectives
  And attenuated columns, on whose cornices
  The occasional tragic mask lay askew,
  And here and there a tiny effete chimera
    With a sphinx's smile.

Embellishing the atrium (at considerable cost)
  Were pictures designed to propagate anxiety,
  Pasiphae, for example, or the Bacchantes
  At their frightful worst, also the deaths of heroes,
  Hercules and other worthies *in extremis*,
  Their limbs coated with the gilt of ancient sunshine,
    And craquelure of frost.

The rest was news and vulcanology, villas destroyed,
   Masterpieces lost – and then of course the populace,
Buried, poor things, under words like ash and pumice
When the wasps of sulphur colonized their lungs.
As for us, we turned our attention elsewhere,
Finding new ways to keep the precincts beautiful
   And idle hands employed.

When the Car Gave Up the Ghost

When the car gave up the ghost outside Lahore
It would have been around a hundred and twenty
In the shade, had there been any shade for sale.
What were for sale were bottles of sugary drinks
And lurid sweetmeats, carried on tricycles
And touted by smiling hyperactive boys,
Who must have been magicked into existence
Out of some conjurer's reappearing trick.
Exchanges were at something near a shout,
When a lineman closed the crossing gates
And the overnight train for Jacobabad,
Nearly brought to its knees by hangers-on,
Ground its way over in maroon and dust.
By then I knew I'd missed my rendezvous.

Flashes in the occipital lobe like star shells
Light up the traces of all this exotica,
Jolting me back to latitude fifty-one.
In a skiff varnished for the silly season
I drift down a macintosh-coloured stream,
Past the green umbrellas of the angling club,
Brooding on roach, past warnings of weirs
And unexplained scuffles in the reed-beds
To a boathouse where the Bloomsbury set
Is said to have engaged in private horseplay.
The slatted gates stand open, ripples and flotsam
Slop against the steps, which I descend,
Clutching my loincloth, bending down to scoop
The sacred waters over my thinning hair.

The Word-Doctor

There are some who gather together in bands
To practise what they believe to be magic,
Self-impaled on pin-sharp broomsticks and cantrips;
And others whose slyly contrived assemblings
Are a cover for undermining brains and glands.

If I am not invited to such affairs
It may be because of words I have uttered
And their edges and qualities as mirrors
(Or specula, as we say in the trade),
And their melt-water dripping unawares.

Some words hang as icicles from the eaves
Of sentences spoken to cover silence,
Some accumulate in the manner of snowflakes,
Lying like a quilt over fishy thoughts,
And there are kinds that flutter down like leaves,

And where they will land is anyone's guess.
Using words is different from using bodies.
Words are flags waving along the frontiers
Of authoritarian states. Some think
The true vocabulary is that of chess.

In part it's a measure of self-defence
Somewhere between the reasoned and instinctive
To ward off poisoners and phoney warlocks.
What's more, it works. Observe me in the desert,
Gazing towards the east, alone, immense.

Who Goes There?

Painted with clots of ochre, black and pipeclay,
The face on my shield is meant to confuse –
The brambly eyebrows, waterfall moustache
And the eyes, dry but with diamond highlights,
Seeming to mesmerize and accuse.

Behind it (the Romans called it a scutum)
I stand with pole-axe and misericorde,
Narrow blade ready for the *coup de grâce*,
At least in theory. On the *qui vive*, of course,
But far less likely to be stabbed than bored.

What I can see of your shield enchants me
When I peep out to check on no-man's-land –
The full-length image, almost three-dimensional,
The ogee curve of your mulberry lip,
The kiss-curl, the language of the hand.

Congratulations on hiding the hatchet
Deep in the folds of your fichu, not revealed
Before the body search; in this unlike
Your dog or talbot or whatever you call
That thing with fangs, which does not bear a shield.

A First Run-Through

Your cue is the clap of thunder.
There you are, framed in the first-floor doorway,
Lurching forward on to the landing
To clatter down stone stairs in your sandals,
Habit flying, girdle in the air,
Missal in the grip of whitened knuckles,
While an amplified voice from the flies
Intones a passage about abyssal depths
And how the cold of the deep ocean
Intrudes under temperate pleasantries.

You exit fearfully stage left
And we hear you somewhere in the wings,
Howling confusedly in dog-Latin.
Handfuls of words reach us — *peccavi* . . .
Damnosa haereditas . . . timor mortis . . .
A brief pause, hints of tumult,
And then — forte from the start — you scream,
Your stretched voice rising, rising, choking,
At the ultimate reach of lungs and throat.

Five seconds later you reappear,
Crawling, half stripped, lit by a red spot,
And drag yourself across the floor,
One leg seemingly amputated,
The boards smeared with what looks like blood.
You retch and moan and inch your way forward,
Getting just as far as centre stage
Where you expire after repeated spasms.
— Yes, it's a small part, a cameo really,
But I'm sure you can make something of it.

A Time for Blushing

For Joan

Plain-clothes inspectors are operating in this store,
In this station and these offices, on every floor.

Dog is reportedly eating dog at the street corners
And television crews focus on the griefs of mourners,

But the inspectors are using listening devices
To harken to the angels calling the starting prices.

Like lymph, they lead shadowy lives, keeping out of sight,
And, like phagocytes, they are always in the right.

Sometimes we may spot them in alcoves, transmitting orders
Or murmuring into miniature tape recorders.

From attics above the bankers' plaza and its fountains,
Encrypted reports go to antennae on the mountains.

They move amongst us unnoticed, in lovat and fawn,
Catching us when we order a drink or mow the lawn.

From lairs in mock orange and dogwood, spectacled eyes
Interpret my movements, read my lips and note my lies,

And remotely controlled bees employ their working hours
Dictating my sins into the corollas of flowers.

The poplars flap their tongues on the far side of the wall,
And the plain-clothes inspectorate overhears it all.

So it's silence for us, my love, it's silence in bed –
And what I was about to say had better not be said.

Sound Waves

When we saw our leader running, we all started to run
Flat out through the shopping centre, soles flopping on terrazzo,
Our heads turning from side to side in mutual enquiry.

And the noise – were we running away from it or towards it?
Had it come from within the woods or out of the woodwork?
Was it the outcry of something dying or giving birth?

Commandeered by whatever was afoot, we ran like foxhounds
And soon we'd know whether to laugh or cry or stand aghast,
But for now it was all uncertainty and kinaesthesia.

The yacht club sat impassively over rubbers of bridge,
Up on the hillside the recesses among granite boulders
Were inscrutable as the mouse-holes that fascinate cats,

And the boarded-up houses where they said travellers squatted
Had masking tape over their mouths, reticent like old clothing
Jettisoned at night during who knows what kinds of imbroglio.

Faltering to a confused stop at the foot of the combe,
We could sense that the quarry had given us all the slip
When the lioness, our leader, sent us back to our homework.

But whatever she said, we knew that the air had been stirred
By an utterance that none of us on our own could bear,
Though as a pack we could persuade ourselves that dark was light.

Or that, at least, is the way I tell myself I remember it.
Pressed on detail, the evidence shows marks of wear and tear,
With frayed edges and a child's unsureness about auxiliaries.

Dublin Zoo 1930

The flow of saliva cheers me up
Once I can hear the iron wheels
Of Mr Flood's galvanized barrow
Rumbling on the cement and catch
The whiff of horse-flesh on the turn.
Like the other assistant keepers
He works with a fag between his lips.

Levering up the gate a hand's-breadth,
He hooks a joint of knacker's meat
On the prongs of his heavy trident
And forces it into the cage
While I snatch and grab at the opening.
Beyond the partition my mate
Is snarling over a blade-bone.

Thanks be for the bars. Worse than dogs
Are the pale-faced packs in motley
And the young ones screeching like peacocks.
On the farther side of the hedge
A mad voice cries 'Off with their heads'
And soon I'll hear the Red Queen's footstep,
Thump thump along the gravel walk.

Their gaze settles on me like pesticide –
And on the absent-minded sex-life
Of rhesus monkeys, and the gait
Of Sundry, the Indian elephant
With her widow's eyes, as she pads
Over the asphalt on command,
Giving jaunts in a crimson howdah.

History Period

The Albatross side-slipped, dived out of the sun
and zoomed up under the belly of the Camel,
Spandaus spouting lead.

They all copied Max Immelmann's half-roll
off the top of the loop.
The gunner with the Lewis had half a chance,

but the twin Vickers spilled their seed over no-man's-land.
The gloved hand on the cockpit's leather-bound coaming
lifted in mocking salute.

Wings were doped soon after sun-down,
ready for fresh ammo and chocks-away at dawn.
They were early birds in the Circus.

The roar of their motors drowns out Mr Glynn
on the Flight of the Earls or the Holy Roman Empire.
(There are two kinds of history, Irish and European.)

On the rough notebook left hand shelters right
and its colouring pencils, red and blue for roundels,
black for the Maltese Crosses.

Eros is sore backwards, and live is evil:
discuss in the passive voice,
drawing on what you have learned

about monastic regimes.
Responses on one side of a clean sheet
to reach Miss Schulz by six on Saturday.

And in the darkness, helmeted and goggled,
the floorboards creak under flying boots,
and O it's the Red Baron! I come! I come!

Age Twelve

Eating rashers and beans
In Woolworth's cafeteria,
Thinking of three-speed gears
Or perhaps of James Stewart
(Certainly not of you,
Rusticated for Lent
In the drizzle and pasture
Of County Carlow's farmland),
I saw you at the counter,
Sliding your tray along,
Not in your dark green gymslip
But a cable-stitch jumper
And not too modest skirt.

Laid-back today, ironic,
I live with unsurprises,
But then my heart, no, diaphragm,
Was jolted from below
As if a whale had surfaced
In waters off Cape Clear,
Showed its encrusted flanks
And slowly resubmerged
Into a flux of foam —
Undreamt-of elemental
Making its presence felt.

I was unseen, invisible,
Anything to avert
The artificial lightning
And removal of bandages.
Time enough for the first steps
On stiff legs in the laboratory.

A Lover's Complaint

For your sake I endured Chinese burns
And never revealed your middle name.

When you arrived late at Departures,
I smiled and swallowed my reproaches,

But aspirin was all I had to offer
The day you lost control in the cable-car.

You whinge about being loved for your body,
Yet your mind is a druse lined with crystals.

Do not think of us as a flight of doves
That wheel in sunshine before settling

Impulsively, with a flurry of wings,
On the corrugations of a tiled dome

Within which Pantocrator stares down
On His unsuspecting congregation.

For the present we are meat and bone.
Time consumes us like a hungry dog.

The Lives of the Cousins

For Maeve Black

The snaps are in black and white, of course,
Few captions, the album-covers scuffed,
But Kitty and Joyce still smile their smiles
From a speedboat tethered by stone steps
In what has the look of a Swiss lake.
One page on and Derek at a picnic
Strains facetiously to draw a cork,
And General Sawyer in dinner jacket
Poses by the rear door of a Daimler.
(It was he who without explanation
In a late codicil to his will
Left me an old-fashioned naval spyglass,
Presumably for looking at stars.
But I have never been a stars person,
Preferring to train my objective
On the bay windows across the townland.)
Hermione and Julius on a cruise
Fill several sheets – games on the boat-deck
And eager Arabs in djellabiyas
Pestering the tourists at Port Said.
Then to badminton at Cowes, and drinks
On Graham's destroyer in the Solent.

It was not like that – nor is it now –
In New Ross or the herbaceous valleys
That trail down from Carlow and Kilkenny,
Where the livestock stand dumbly around
Under broad-leaved trees in the demesnes
And the Nore slides swiftly over crowfoot.
In these parts there is not much call

For cigarette-holders or shady hats.
The creamery coughs from before dawn
And all day the foreigners' meat lorries
Rumble and thud along the main street.
Though I shoot with a couple of Councillors
And the Principal of the Tech,
A brace of woodcock is small return
For hours of damp shoulders and cold feet.
But asylum resides in the office —
Virginia-creepered, shabby but warm —
Where my pink-cheeked secretary sits
Typing out conveyances and wills.
Drinking my morning coffee, I observe
Her bosom snug in Botany wool
And her reassuringly thick legs.

Ancestors and Refugees

I

The dog's mercury has come early this year,
As it did last year and for some years before that —
A hot trickle through the capillaries
Into the embarrassment of spring.
And, mensch, what a meal people make of it!

Out of nineteen live births the first to survive
Until the age of twelve was number four.
That was in the eighteen twenties and thirties,
A testimony, sort of, to routine
And elasticity of animal spirits.

The generations overlapped like slates.
When she was in the mood, Mary Louisa
Dandled Frances, her biological aunt;
And the newly born were named in memory
Of brothers and sisters not so long deceased.

The illnesses that took them by the throat
Had names and crises and were borne
With the aid of biblical apologetics,
Though after Whit God was allowed a break
And hay fever was called 'a summer cold'.

But physiology kept their numbers up.
As raindrops fell off the black buds of ash,
Draining into gutters, the survivors found
The feather-bed a refuge from the drawing-room
Where grandfather read aloud from Walter Scott.

Despite the foxed engravings and the smell
Of mouldy plaster, hearth and home were clean,
Though Anne's lace collar may have been slightly soiled,
Just as it was last Sunday, because O'Neill's
Had run out of superior yellow soap.

'Allens' mill is grinding wheat' sang the children
Who dawdled homeward from Miss Duggan's school,
Stopping to peg a stone into the stream
That turned our obsolescent wheel and ground
The family's fortunes into liquidation.

II

A century later came the refugees,
Arriving in the playground during break,
Mystifying, like pods from outer space.
One week a schoolboy, next a youngish woman,
Teleported in on the Quaker lifeline.

The children of real or so-called communists
Straight out of illustrations to Eric Kästner,
And one or two Jews, force-fed into maturity,
They stood surrounded by armoured luggage,
Trying to look as though they were not at sea.

In belted jackets and thick specs and leather,
They struggled to get their tongues around exile.
'Kreuzberg', they said, or 'Oranienstrasse',
Not sure whether these were answers to questions
No one had thought to ask.

Wavy-haired Kurt, an arrogant seventeen
Cast away amongst the unknowing provincials,
Had a protruding navel and crossed swords,
Unwisely, with the mathematics master
On some issue of hygiene or propriety,

With thunder-flashes banging on past bedtime.
Unable to blank off the foreign tantrums,
The dormitory lay hypnotized and abashed
At overhearing what should not have been heard.
And gossips were saying that Kurt knew about women,

When he softly and suddenly vanished away.
But Georg, thirteen, was a tolerated bull-calf,
Though his name defeated rain-softened larynxes.
Buoyant except at nightfall, he fooled with language,
'Ach du meine Güte!' and 'Du Esel!'

Breaking up his passages of cobbled English.
Käthe was older and gave one-to-one
Tuitions in Goethe, when her braids and earphones
Were uneasy reminders of Margarethe.
Puritanical, she took exception to 'nackt'.

The Poles came later, like capricious horses,
But by then impatience was in the air
And curvetting temperaments like Peter's
Were an invitation to practical jokes –
And of course the fencing lessons were a mockery.

III
Treasuring a picture postcard of the Vistula,
Peter, with slowing body chemistry, learned
To capitalize on a profile like Novello's;
And Käthe married a man from the North,
Whom, no doubt, she managed with her sulks.

Georg made a success of spun concrete pipes,
His children have the local twang and farmers
Applaud his man's-man speeches at the Rotary.
Berlin's imprisoned in his snowing paperweight
And a snap of mother smiling by the Wannsee.

Photographs get muddled with wisps of dreams,
Undated letters, expressions of endearment
Spoken by who-knows-whom and heard in years
For which our visas are no longer valid.
Even the consular section is out of bounds.

Wide lowland rivers are much of a muchness,
Silt-laden water curls past the pontoons,
The barges grew up in the school of hard knocks
And the passenger train that clanks twice daily
Across the red-leaded girder bridge

Might be on its way to Cork or Breslau.
On the farther bank, when you can make it out,
There is something funny about the flags
They choose to fly – faded or upside down
Or waving incomprehensible emblems.

Smoke rises continually from their chimneys
And they rarely if ever look in our direction.
What we take to be street signs are illegible,
Even through the high-powered binoculars
That give us glimpses of their old-fashioned cars.

It will not have escaped you that the trains
Run only from east to west, and those on board
Look doped and never peer out of the windows.
I once, aged fourteen, attempted to cross on foot,
Stepping from sleeper to sleeper, but the drop

To the sliding waters brought on my vertigo.
Their atmosphere is years thick, their colours muted,
Unlike these sap-green evaginated shoots
Of dog's mercury on the fast march forward,
Disregarding calls for self-restraint.

It must be the Oder, mensch, or something like it
That keeps the lot of us at sixes and sevens.
Meanwhile I stand by for a call on the intercom,
Saying that a visitor in a stocking mask
Has arrived and waits for me at reception.

Kerry

Low tide at Glenbeigh,
The sands shine like steel,
Air from Greenland streaks over
Ten furlongs of wet mineral –
Terrain of worms and molluscs
Where what is laid is hatched.
Twice a day the tide's hand
Wipes out the tracks of crabs
Hastening *sur les pointes*.

Visitors in thin shoes
Back off for tea and seed-cake
In the Bay Hotel,
Set like an old molar
In the hillside's bracken,
The paint thick and white,
Brass locks and handles
Buffed into silence,
Where middle-aged women
Who could speak about loss
Smilingly feed the fire
And plump the cushions.
A sprawling labrador
Looks back over his shoulder
And tail-thuds the carpet
For not yet easy newcomers
Who breathe the warmth and handle
Magazines about horses.

Inland by shelving margin
A willowy schoolboy
Peels off his grey-green jersey
To trace a downward arc
Like half-seen leaping salmon,
Diving white as stripped twig
Into tea-brown lake-water
Where tunnels made by trout
Are collapsing into wakes
Devoid of trace or image.

A man of unclear purpose
In worn but bespoke tweeds
And a hat like a prune
Records the boy's passage
On a half-plate camera
From the turn of the century,
An image that will surface
In a red-lit private room.

Lemon juice, milk and urine
Work as invisible inks,
Rusty longhand showing up
Shaky and feint on paper
Held close to smouldering wood.

Head sunk in pillow
Between lights-out and cock-crow,
The pulse within my ear
Counts down the digits
All the way to zero.

Wildlife Park from Train

They were larger than foxes but smaller than cows
Or, to bring the scene into slightly sharper focus,
Shorter than donkeys but inches taller than sheep.
Matt in texture, they seemed to be covered in hair
(Though this was not something we could put to the test)
And their colour, too, was difficult to pin down,
Never within shouting distance of black or white,
But a brown or grey it was hard to put a name to.
Their heads (if indeed those were heads, not tails) were poised
On average at about the height of a trough.
A few appeared to graze, while others stared around,
Perhaps keeping a weather eye open for predators;
And as to their orientation on the grassland,
With some exceptions it was roughly east-to-west.
As a way of living it looked like a soft berth
Where the tacit injunctions were to eat one's fill,
But also to go quietly when the time came.

On the Quay

Soon after nightfall the octopus-boat
Creeps over the bay on kerosene lights,
Bright and sharp, as though through reversed binoculars.

Gliding without bow-wave, the hunters float,
Hot eyes glare down and itch for tip of tentacle.
A genre subject for Joseph Wright of Derby.

But this is the Aegean in July;
Voices droning over brandy behind us
And the short hiss of the coffee machine

Drown what might be an underwater cry
Breaking out of a crevice in the limestone.
Was that a splash? Is that a bundle hoisted?

Here we are all ephemeral as foam,
Shallow outlanders, in this world not of it.
Why get steamed up about its blameless cephalopods?

There's plenty to fret about nearer home,
Kingston abattoir, for example, grey,
Like something left over in Eastern Europe.

Journeys

Reading Primo Levi in the park,
And what looked like a full stop
Started to move, paused and set off
Towards the top of the page, as if heading
For Scotland or wherever civilization
Still hung on, though from time to time
It hesitated and veered a wee bit
To right or left, as though sensing a threat
From other cruising periods and commas.
But after weighing up all the signals
Resumed its trek to the northern edge,
Moving (one assumed) on legs, their existence
As dubious as the canals on Mars,
Even under a magnifying glass.

Wind hustled through twigs, the sun went in
And the dot halted, struck by omens.
A striped gunship circled overhead
And filled the sky, chemical weapons
Visible, protruding from tail-end port.
But with heat-seeking eyes on the big time
The black and yellow monster banked,
Accelerated its chitinous fans
And sheered off into summer foliage.

The dot migrated tranquilly on
In the direction of *ultima Thule,*
Then turned, as though heading into the breeze,
Opened infinitesimal elytra
And, extending (one had to suppose)
Wings invisible to the naked eye,
Cast off into the turbulent air
In its quest for the four freedoms.

After the full stop, the English text continued:
On the evening of the fourth day
The cold became intense: the train
Ran through interminable black pine forests,
Climbing perceptibly.

No Turning Back Now

I

Circumspect fingers used to locate the bottle
In the darkness at the back of the cupboard
And, holding it up before a shaded window,
Barely loosen the ground-glass stopper
In its vaselined neck to sanction
The outflow of two or three viscous drops.

These days the fire doors stand open, propped
By the red extinguishers, to speed the movement
Of serum and flour to waiting aircraft,
And all night long over Beowulf's sea
The flocculent cloud base is lit up
Where gas flares off at Balder and Viking.

II

The traders' day begins soon after dawn.
Shining wide-eyed on the looking-glass towers,
The scrubbed and towelled sunlight has forgotten
Yesterday's disappointments and traductions.
(You know, don't you, that the sun drinks at lunchtime?
How else explain the hardboiled stare of nones
And the evening's lachrymose reassurances?)
They measure out their lives with telephones.

New York follows London into darkness
When the usurers' voices are snuffed out,
And ears in need of sleep find messages hidden
In the after-hours breath of the loudspeaker.

Floodlights dazzle the garden when intruders
With stockinged heads blunder into the alarms
With threats to the lords spiritual and temporal
And their daughters' endearing young charms.

III

Ladies and gentlemen, in one of my best tricks
I show you multiplication and division:
First you observe two rabbits; now there are six;
And now there are one thousand and twenty-four.
After the drum-roll I wait for your applause.
Keep moving, ladies and gentlemen, and remember
That a pure number can never be a cause.

There is a grey hill far away where throngs
Of wasting people entertain the flies.
That murmur is the *caput mortuum* of songs
In praise of Aesculapius and Hygeia.
The rains, if they come, will come too late,
Washing the top-soil off into gurgling gullies
To leave a field of stones, a place to wait.

IV

For good or ill, and it seems to be for ill,
The numbers keep on growing larger and larger,
And you think it cannot continue, but it will.

Into the last green policies, one by one,
Rides someone from the Apocalypse on a charger,
Readying himself to do what has to be done.

Holding On

Felted doors divided the anteroom
From the sanctum where unfastidious
Grand seniors prearranged the outcomes.
On our side we fiddled with notebooks,
Awaiting the summons to take down
The latest biddings and directives.

Please pay particular attention
To the passages in italics,
Failure to observe which will carry
A penalty of broken legs
Or at least of localized burns,
Without provision for appeal.

Donations in the form of cheques
Should be crossed 'account payee only'
And made out to the Party's Chairman.
These are taken into consideration,
But should not be bestowed on Sundays
When he is busy eating God.

O maker of burglar alarms,
Be our breastplate against predation.
Before night darkens the estates
Register our souls in your database
And immerse our swollen endowments
In the waters of your safe-keeping.

O tester of condoms, pray for us,
Shield us from unnatural abstinence
And spread your gospel to diminish
The numbers jogging at our gates.
Contain the covetous and caution
Those for whom enough is enough.

O friendly pander, be our guide,
Take us by our soft hands to picnic
In your well-tended arboretum.
Keep your counsel, accept this money
And hold down for our satisfaction
The pleasures that slip through our fingers.

I have been to the crematorium
And come back with my father's dust,
Which I sprinkle around the foot
Of *Magnolia grandiflora,*
Knowing that I can trust my landlord
When the lease comes up for renewal.

Graffiti

I am Balaclava man
My jaw was found in Java
My molars in the Olduvai
And my dental record
In a surgery in Paddington.

One beetle recognises
Another beetle,
And the same is true of stonefish.
But it's first names only –
As it might be Ankh! or Fishface!

I bleed when cut
But do not laugh when tickled.
Peering through my monocular
I observe faces
That could be Balaclavas.

My address is fixed.
I am the slave of the text.
Through a blurred window
I project images
That breed in my sensorium.

Interesting Times

When the pestilence had left Newcastle
We sent in the prisoners of war
As an advance guard to clear the rats
And burn their carcasses on waste land
Between the town and the hills to the north.
And to these dry hills we then despatched
The prisoners, giving them their freedom.
It is not known how many survived
Or what caused the deaths of those who perished.

The burial of our own dead we left
To the old people, arguing fairly
That they had an abundance of memories
And must possess a kind of immunity
To have lived so gradely and so long.
But after the carting and interment
In mass graves, they were required to camp
For six weeks outside the eastern gate.
We were pleased to see how many returned.

The rest of us, except for the wounded,
Small children and women at full term,
Sweated for days on the muddy bankside,
Humping up full buckets from the river
To sluice the filth out of the buildings.
Months later we might still catch the stench.
Few if any sexual relationships
Were brokered or resumed in this period,
But there was a brisk market in commodities.

Electricity has become a legend,
A concept the young ones cannot grasp.
And sometimes we forget to boil the water
Or lack the fuel with which to do so,
Having consumed it in the imperative
To forge new weapons and new defences
From scrap metals of the past regime.
These we render down, though there are alloys
Beyond our ability to melt.

Elsewhere the future may be in progress,
While here traffic makes its way on foot,
Porterage being a sort of livelihood.
The insects having returned to office
With their doctrinaire policies, losing
Is what we appear to be condemned to.
Laws, so-called, are vested in hard hands,
But we pass our nights in fear of pilferers
And our leisure at knuckle-bones and hazard.

A Song for Norway

Today I shall consider the Pelton Wheel,
The principles underlying its design,
Its merits and its shortcomings in relation
To machines engineered for axial flow.
Efficiency, as you know, is the bottom line.

Yesterday I danced on the lake shore at sunset,
Upright and corseted in my inhibition.
I stood by a deathbed in a heated room
Dry-eyed amongst a family in black
Whose deity was more tyrant than magician.

Today I slide on snow and laugh over liquor,
Phenomena come and go at my behest,
I look through glass at the hills, hoarding my selfhood,
While computers redistribute my reserves.
At the end of the day, alchemy is best.

Yesterday I manhandled racks of smoked fish
And kept the stove alive through the month-long night,
Drawn by the enigmas of chlorotic girls,
Whose lamp-black eyes consumed me over prayers
For the drowned and the sinners against the Light.

Searching for different tenses and dimensions,
I dream of a beach bared by a falling tide
Over which unidentified waders scurry –
Like the crowds scattering from the Winter Palace
That October. Precipitate. Untried.

The Surveyor's Story

We left the freighter moored off Zanzibar,
Riding light, with half the crew in cradles
Hammering rust and smearing on poisonous paint
Below the Indian Ocean loading line.

Heading north-west as far as the thorn forest,
We got into arguments about Frobenius,
His standing in the anthropological fraternity
And how he was seen by the Wemba people;

Not having pick-up trucks and cigarettes,
They had read the world with a spiritual dictionary,
Focussing on ancestors and parts of enemies
Parcelled in leaves and kept for a rainy day –

Or so I claimed above the roar of the engine
As we left the red laterite and zigzagged
Up the escarpment to the site, where gneiss
Was making known its views on TNT.

A country's broken bones had been strewn about
For grading and pushing into shapes like roads,
But the yellow machines had died in the sun.
Only the insects seemed to be at work.

Everywhere men were lying around like jacks
Fallen off the back of a ganger's hand,
Faces dusty and eyes dark with dudgeon.
You could smell the telepathy in the air.

When someone snapped open a can of beer,
Kalashnikovs countered from behind the ridge.
Unmeaning barked out of the cabin radio;
Even the tellurometer was kaput.

This was not Siberia, where the Ob
Runs to the Arctic under cover of ice;
Here blood would dribble down open storm-drains
And nourish ticks and leeches.

For us it was out and fast, back to the coast
And its corrupted venues, where we loll
On patios and murder swordfish and lager
And mango ices out of sight of orphans.

Forgive the lapse. Reverting to Frobenius,
In Chapter 32 he distinguishes
Between murder and raids and warfare proper,
The last marking the advanced society.

Time After Time

In between the Kingdoms
    The so-called Intermediate Periods;
Between Chou and Han
    The Period of the Warring States:
The word 'period' lies
    Over such times like camouflage netting
Over a field hospital.
    But at least periods have their endings
As well as beginnings,
    Seasons when buried beans may sprout.
In Central America
    Candles simply guttered and went out.

Catastrophe or period,
    Blackbirds fulfil May-time obligations
Calling among beech-tops
    In slow-motion coloratura,
Oppressed seeds reassert
    Themselves when poisons have drained away,
Even in resolutely
    Inhospitable places, things proceed
With their replication,
    Nematodes and arthropods hold on
To their old possessions,
    And no-one notices that man has gone.

Practical Rain-Making

The Pitt Rivers Museum Revisited

Salisbury Cathedral distilled,
Tested for purity, approved,
Reconstituted in cast-iron
And peopled with rickety skeletons
Of dinosaurs, elephants and bears.

Patter across the tiles and gratings
To reach the old collector's storehouse
And his trove of paraphernalia
From the fear-lined lives of hunters
In blighted hill-tracts, infested bush,
Hot swamps between Cancer and Capricorn,
And the lands of blizzards and wizards.

Animal, vegetable and mineral,
But mostly cinnamon-coloured wood,
And parcels of skin and hair, whose origins
Are best left in their own departments
Of Euclidean space and time.

Hard to see all these odds and ends
As part of diurnal existence –
Feeding the children, keeping clean.
Interned and frail, as though tainted
By long-lived viruses of magic
Spread from furred or dusty fetishes,
There is half a dimension missing.

But not from these paralysed ancestors
Locked in hardwood, their prominent organs
Static but swollen with threat.
It's all about the substance of power
And survival and what is shrunk from.

Drive a heavy nail into the head,
Not all the way, just an inch or so.
There are no sutures, it will not split,
Rain-forest timber has a fine grain.
And never mind the desperate eyeballs,
The figure's pose denotes endurance.
Good, now the pact is beyond question.

After propitiation, rain
Will fall from the sieve of the clouds
If you keep your side of the bargain:
Sacrifice a chicken, eat no meat,
Be continent, do not touch your wife.

Sometimes it worked, sometimes it didn't.
Nowadays on the crazed clay
Of what was once the bed of a lake
Lizards unpredictably dash
Into and out of dark fissures
And groups of prescient mice
Are filling their stomachs with seeds
That have lost the will to go on.
But most of them lack the nous
To keep their heads and voices down
When cameramen and presenters
Fall out of the waterless sky.

Imperial War Museum, November

Podium and Ionic propylaeum,
Symbol of public-school civilization
Built post-Waterloo on the site of Bedlam,
Jaws of the keepers' world and that odd blend
Of machines and apology and pride.

Inside is movement, arbitrary as ants',
Where children with their immoderate gestures
Put yesterday's pecking orders to the test,
While unknown to themselves they store on file
Memories programmed like dragons' teeth.

Gatling, Vickers-Armstrong, Supermarine:
The notices instruct us not to touch,
For fear our fingers might be sensitized
By the thin glaze of suffering and animus
That coats all this armourers' stock-in-trade.

The sun aims sideways, under and beyond
The strong-arm stuff of the fifteen-inch guns,
And, against the fumes of the Lambeth Road,
Shows spots of pink and yellow where absent-minded
Roses have gone to sleep with their lights burning.

Metaphors and Indians

Here come the constellations of words.
Boys I knew clambered up pines and palms
For ospreys' eggs or neighbours' fibrous coconuts.
Part of the fun was in the climbing,
But also in were grazes and contusions,
Giddiness, the gravity of gravity.
I exercised caution on the ground,
Pleading an undescended testicle.

Later on I tried my hand with kites,
Galloping up the brow of the hill,
Hands full of pessimism and string,
While the gimcrack frameworks wheeled,
Took fright and nosed-dived to the grass.
It was asking too much of old constructions –
And those were last year's cones on stiff twigs,
Moving above *Mare nostrum*'s foam.

Sheltering a struck match, Tiger Brand,
I touched it to the loose ends of statements
That flared and writhed and levitated
Up to the ceiling, frail and friable
As ashes of amaretti paper,
Or floated like night-lights on the river
To disappear miles down among mangroves
And mud-banks alive with crustaceans.

Steam-heating and the windows immoveable,
Painted shut against the outside world,
And the hotel's velvets pink with fatigue,
Drapes and tassels limp as catkins.
A duvet offered me a Turkish night,
But if they'd thought I'd sweat it out
The money-men found me refractory.
Not a word was to pass my Cupid's bow.

I saw forcemeat wriggle from the mincer,
Falling in red worms spotted with fat,
Haphazardly, bodies in a clearing,
The earth shovelled back before nightfall
And men slipping away between the birches.
But May brought the usual primroses,
Amaryllis did not erupt
Like four loudspeakers on a pole.

Cold-shouldered by the divining-rod,
A dew-pond was my last investment,
Limestone slabs sloping to a cistern
Where droplets from dream-work could assemble
And help the rose-chafers, green and shining,
To complete their metamorphoses
And decorate flower-heads of thistles,
Undisturbed by the academies.

Car-Boot Sale

The faded colours of a chairback
Crewelled in the suburbs of Bad Ems
About the time of Edward VIII,
The gift of an admiring alien
To the late Mrs Hopford-Kirk,
Relict and *grande dame* of this parish,
Now for sale from the open boot
Of a grass-green 1980s Peugeot,
Parked, to cover eventualities,
Nose out in a buttercup meadow,
The freehold of the Church Commissioners,
Assigned for use in perpetuity
To the benefit of St Olave's,
This wording interpreted flexibly
By the present worldly incumbent,
One of whose forebears was last man
To be winched by breeches buoy
From the SS *Alexander Yeats*,
Out of Savannah with a cargo
Of pitch-pine, driven on the rocks
Off Gurnards Head by a storm Force 10
Sweeping ESE from Cape Farewell,
The sepia print fading to yellow,
But mounted in a silver frame,
Thin as paper, distinctly marked
H, with the irony of an anchor,
Birmingham, 1882,
When Lady Rossiter unveiled
The new East window in St Olave's,
A flush of ruby glass and azure,
In memory of Jack, her boy,

Put to the sword in Afghanistan,
The posthumously awarded medal
A sleepy grey in the light of tea-time
And of eyes estimating flatware,
Fittings, the combings of a guest-house
That died on its feet with its owner,
Formerly in the world of tin,
Mr Penhallow, fond of donkeys,
With whom he had something in common,
A talent for standing unmoved
At the panic of bells and sirens,
Keeping his balance on the slope
Of a vibrating table, wet
And streaming, while grains of quartz
Parted company with cassiterite,
And dank shafts followed the lode
Steeply under the sea from Kurnow
And the fulmar wheeled on stiff wings,
Glassy-eyed, a triumph of taxidermy,
The cracked case easily repaired
By glazier with rule and diamond,
Likewise the picture-glass enclosing
That what-was-it-called RA winner,
Keen eyes, a finger pointing west,
It points for thee and television
And the gathering in the counthouse.

In Memoriam

A look in a convex mirror would have told him
What he needed to know just then about space and time,
His own Cyrano image retreating into both
With the haste of a cinematic spacecraft,
The lips and ears exhibiting a bluish tint.
But it seems he was more like a cat than a peacock.
Facts about aneurysm and the circle of Willis
Had been laid down in his memory like a vintage,
Not to be broached, but passed on to his children,
Who would duly receive and cradle them in their cellars
Or under the stairs with tricycles and dusters
Till someone dared to suggest a public auction.
It wasn't that the medicine man had spilled the beans
About the causes of funerals, or had conjured up
Helen and Paris out of eddies of pagan smoke,
Rather that hurdles were there to be leapt
And banks to be broken.
                          Turning to hail a taxi,
Messages from his pulse had been shouted down
By a siren being rushed to intensive care
With the rending of veils and the hubris of servants.
In some respects Cape Wrath is a haven of peace.
An unemployed gymnast could have stood in for him
On the day assigned for the tumble on the stairs,
But nobody was around to take the call,
The outer office having gone for an early lunch
(Cottage cheese, white wine and a small banana).
Not, of course, that Atropos would have changed her mind,
Given her gift for extempore solutions
Like conjuring up black ice at the drop of a hat.
Melancholy, yes, but the tonality of Then

Depends so much on what is understood by Now –
Like the advertisement for the house on the promontory
Where he used to wipe his shoes on *Cave Canem*.

The Task

With work in progress I barely doze at night,
Then flitter around the garden from first light
For stuff to build with, grasses and marl and hair.
What tensions, I wonder, can the structure bear
As I prod among the crooked twigs and pull
Experimentally at a strand of wool.
Sometimes I hang head down in order to fix
A twist of moss among intractable sticks
While a nervy wind fidgets through every hole.
The chemistry of fatigue softens the soul,
All sorts of dangers, around, above, below,
Haunt the indifferent not-self, and I know
That art is a fabrication to divide
The dark exterior from the dark inside.

Bee Talk

She asked for a poem about flowers,
Chromatic, indulgent to the retina,
After all those inner city images
Of men who don't know right from wrong
     Or theirs from ours.

Insects might take a more jaundiced view.
Confronted by the sexual appetite
Of *Antirrhinum majus*, the snapdragon,
Even a bumble bee's conditioned reflex
     Might go askew.

First the sulphur-yellow, streaked with wine,
Then landing on the pouting lower lip
Of a closed mouth asking to be entered,
And heaving the pellicle up on furred shoulders
     To reach the shrine.

It shuts behind you, as your tail withdraws
Into the translucent coloured cell
With its possibly infective mites,
Where you rummage around in the nectary
     With tongue and claws

For a soupçon of sugary juice
(Someone, it seems, has been here before you),
And all the time the struggle with anthers
And their suffocating orange dust,
     Sticky, profuse,

Muffling antennae, stinging the eyes,
Coating the hairs of abdomen and legs.
Come on out of the arsenic mines,
You little goose, observe the shorter days,
The autumn skies.

Pond-Life

For Ted Hughes

The Latin takes your hand,
Keeping you on the rails
In the murk of the pond bottom,
Where a creature removes its face before dinner,
Mask hinging downwards from the mouth-parts
To consume *Daphnia*,
The water flea of glass.

Aeshnea juncea is still a nymph,
Moving to her goal of dragon-powered flight
With a nymph's appetite
And a roc's ambition.
Sinbad will have allure
In the granules of her Fabergé eyes,
But now she settles for *Cyclops*.

Nepa, the water scorpion,
Comes on like a dead leaf,
But for the front legs, which close like penknives;
Nonetheless avoids the larger worms,
Hirudo, say, with medical applications,
More contractile than the horse leech
And with sharper teeth.

Do not pay the waterboatman,
And it's *sauve qui peut*
When the heron's bill
Smashes through the silver ceiling.
But up here on terra firma
Your hawk was not *Accipiter* to anyone
And the little foxes were never *Vulpes vulpes*.

Frogs and Fishes

The get-up of South American tree frogs
Cocks a snook at the conventions of art —
Glaucous and glairy, with their random blotches
Of lime green or so-called 'apple', in shapes
That infringe the copyright of amoebae,
And making no attempt to touch the heart.

Tropical fish, of course, are even worse,
With meretricious names like Regal Tang,
Harlequin Sweetlip and Neon Goby.
Slickly curved, tricked out in modish colours,
Theirs is the world of bibelots and kitsch,
Glib assertions in decorators' slang.

Against all these, the externals of birds
Speak of designers with a sense of style.
And we cannot question the taste of insects,
Outlandish, perhaps, but never vulgar,
Frozen in their archaic forms and postures,
One foot forward, the lips a not quite smile.

But that's just talk to keep the flies of silence
From settling on my hands and lips and eyes,
The hankering to chip off bits of chaos,
Flake by flake, word by word, and disengage
What might have been a poem from the clinging
Gangue of insistent voices, grunts and cries.

There are poems that resemble tree frogs
And others like the Sunburst Butterfly fish,
But verses really look better in feathers,
As in the aesthetic of the red kite,
Or come to that in the guise of cicadas
Whose shrilling makes whatever sense you wish.

Inside Arabia

The inhabitants of the Empty Quarter
Sleep much of the day and move by night,
Stepping out from behind the breasts of sand-dunes
To resume the tête-à-têtes whose forgotten
Difficult-to-pin-down beginnings lie
In leftovers from usage and event,
Bones piled on the rim of the *plat du jour*.

Questions about the way to the Fertile Crescent
Are met with smiles and humbug about camels
And tradition and the lack of markers.
But saddled transport seems to come and go
At near enough the appointed times,
Theatrical bargaining fills the evenings
And at full moon the haggled-over bales
Can be seen lurching away into the uplands.

Overflown by migrating storks,
We have to hang about for our guides —
Shadowy characters apt to materialize
Smiling from the shelter of night-cold rocks,
Who could all do with lessons in voice production
Or simple specifics against catarrh
And the hawking and spitting behind the tents.

But insofar as a message emerges
The tone is neutral, some might say teasing.
The granaries of the nomads are all around,
Their latitudes and longitudes a food
For the constantly baffled numerologist
Seated under the doum-palm with his abacus.
The problem is fine-tuning the dowsing-rod
To the vibrations of rice, wheat, sorghum, maize.

Sunday

Today I shall name names.
Yesterday I named animals,
And the day before that,
Taking things in their sequence,
I named the birds and fishes.
My naming of the plants
Took place some two days earlier,
As I had to make time
To name sun, moon and stars,
Which, through an oversight,
I missed out on day three.
But today, while I rest,
I intend to name names.

Sympathy and *compassion*
Would do as names, if only
I could think of a use for them;
Justice might come in handy,
Though when I'm not quite sure,
And the same goes for *liberty*.
But *suffering* and *grief*
Look to be sound constructions
And of wide application.
I am doubtful if *beauty*
Would serve any real purpose
And remain very much
In two minds about *God*.

Much more to my taste
Are labels that summon
Presences to the mind –
No-nonsense names like those
Coined in the week just past:
Python, custard apple, pig,
Date palm, clay and *salt.*
I relish *smoke* and *poppy*
And, for a bit of fun,
Shall nominate the *fossils.*
But I have not succumbed
To concepts or decided
What makes the world go round.

Cloud Cover

Our caterpillar crossed the Sea of Crises,
Turned lunar south and crawled over ejecta
On the cratered fields of Fertility.
Later we moved on to the Sea of Moisture,
Pitching our shiny aluminium tent
On its floor of incoherent dust.

Over the sawtooth skyline lay the *Mare Frigoris*
And way beyond that the *Lacus Mortis*
(For graveyard names we retain the Latin),
Though it was less than a day's slow driving
To the *Lacus Somniorum* or Lake of Dreams,
Which can hardly be referred to with a straight face.

Overhead to be stared at was our terracentre,
The full-face discus coated with verdigris,
Wall-eyed, autistic or disingenuous.
There, we could see, was the advertised Pacific,
But elsewhere lay shifting jalousies of cloud,
Behind which who knows what went on.

Map Reference SU41

No nonsense about the names of the old farms –
Coldharbour, Flint, Folly, Starveall, even Skeleton;
Few fantasizing addresses like Barleypark,
Mount Pleasant or Meadow (smiling into mirrors).
Nor was there much cheer in holdings called Lonesome,
Roughdown and Hardwell; resignation, presumably,
Or justified self-pity, some sort of irony
Or recognition of the skin-cracking chalk
That kept insinuating chunks of its spine
Through the coat of washed-out weatherings and grit.
Maps as communal headstones, portable altars.

What was yielded could barely be called a living
And bad teeth, bronchitis, the dread of diphtheria
And the tussle with blood-poisoning and whitlows,
Not to mention contagion among the sheep
And crops affected by rust or dieback, jaded
The farmers' manhood and their partners' complaisance.
But they soldiered on in the wet north-westerlies
With smouldering infections, and fingerstalls
Issued free of charge by the local dispensary,
And accidents – a foot impaled on a tine –
Meant carbolic, oiled silk, bandages and prayer.

Of course there were breaks in the cloud cover; creatures
Now relegated to no-man's-land or science
Made wary visitations – the weather eyes
Of stone curlew flat among tussocks, a harrier
Transiting fast and low across the warrens;
But naturalists on the whole they were not.
So you can keep your *nostalgie de la boue*.
'Yes, yes, all that is taken as read,' you cry,

Pulling smoothly off on to a picnic site
In a motor car littered with toys and guidebooks,
'Today's occupiers have today's anxieties
And, like us, assume the dark glasses of anomie'.

The Factotum

After the misfortune of his master's death,
The uppity children, the contested will,
He barricaded himself into his memory
And conversed only with outriders of God.
The doctor's questions were a waste of breath.

He had checked the boundary for gaps and set
Tiaras of broken glass on tops of walls,
The garden was never short of blood or bonemeal,
Hinges were oiled, the cars reflected vanity,
His ledgers set the pride against the debt.

But overnight the scenery had been changed,
The spots were brighter, noises off more piercing
And the words, when he could hear them, were familiar,
But seemed to have acquired different meanings.
He and his milieu had become estranged.

Now that dramas were resolved and fences mended
Without his keys or spanners or advice,
He could see the harsh crescendi of applause,
Though never meant for him, were all in honour
Of stirring effects that he had not intended.

The young in-laws were charming, no one was rude,
But old immutables were scorched by new regimes
And eyes made out his future with their glances.
Laid up in rooms above the former coach-house,
His fancies grew grotesque, his logic skewed,

Sometimes he wondered where he was and why.
When things got disconnected from their names
The rest home drew him like a pavement artist.
Up at the house some friends arrived for lunch.
A grandchild stretched its hand to grab a fly.

Fleeced

In the crook of the hill
He held her hotly
With his sheep-shearer's hand.
Beyond the hedge
Trucks and transporters rolled,
Growling in procession
To the dockside ramp
And the gaping sea doors
Of the ro-ro ferry.

All these obvious symbols —
Things standing in
For other things
And not for themselves —
Make me want to throw up.
I have ceased to guffaw
At speeded-up movies
Of factory chimneys
Falling and uprising.

It was my bottle-fed ewe
That was shorn and shivered
And now thinks herself wise
In her felted undercoat.
There are tears to cry with
And lies to speak with.
I must turn away,
Being Job's comforter
Without electuary.

Stowing it in the cellar
Among the suitcases
With broken handles,
I am the doomster,
The suffered loudmouth
At the committee
Or the fool at the paseo
Parading a bad-tempered
Leopard on a string.

Way Back Then

The floor-show ends, lights dim, I tilt the bottle;
The maestro turns, vibrant in black and white,
Confers the boon of his electric ego
And drives the music forward through the night.

So here I sit, champagne glass in my hand,
Afloat on rhythms of the Latin south,
Drawn by inexorable tidal currents
To the pearl harbour of your smiling mouth.